The Light Inside

Elizabeth Turnbull

AuthorHouse™
1663 Liberty Drive
Bloomington, IN 47403
www.authorhouse.com
Phone: 1-800-839-8640

Published by AuthorHouse 2/3/2012

ISBN: 978-1-4685-4175-5 (sc)

Library of Congress Control Number: 2012900448

Any people depicted in stock imagery provided by Thinkstock are models,
and such images are being used for illustrative purposes only.
Certain stock imagery © Thinkstock.

This book is printed on acid-free paper.

Because of the dynamic nature of the Internet, any web addresses or links contained in this book may have changed
since publication and may no longer be valid. The views expressed in this work are solely those of the author and do not
necessarily reflect the views of the publisher, and the publisher hereby disclaims any responsibility for them.

author HOUSE®

This book is dedicated to my sister-in-law Roseita, my husband Craig and the brilliant lights in our lives Gerry, Laurie, Leanna' Mae, Angelina and Nicolas

Further acknowledgement and gratitude is also given to Marcia Kirton in support of her work for children's charities

If you would like to contact Marcia she can be reached at mhkirton@yahoo.com

You were born
with a *light* inside,
and from the moment
I saw you my *heart*
filled with pride.

I'll hold you and kiss you
and bathe you with care,
then snuggle you close
when we rock in the chair.

From your very first *sounds*
to your very first steps,
I'll watch in *amazement*
at what will come next.

The *first* time you fall
and cry in despair,
I'll *hug* you and promise
to always be there.

I'll **dust** you off
and put you
on course,
to **tackle**
all footstools
and tables
by force.

You will not give up but hold to your path,
Until you walk freely
with a bright, fun filled laugh.

Your light will grow brighter with each passing day, and stay in you warmly when tears come your way.

As time marches on
and parties abound,
You'll have so much love
from all those around.

Presents will
come and many
a toy, as I watch
your *happiness*
and feel all
your *joy!*

When **learning** to ride, to read and to swim, when climbing a **tree** to hang from its limb.

Much joy will come and great blessings too, while my faith never wavers in all you can do.

Playtime will be there as friends call your name, and you'll run with your light to be part of their game.

YOUR LIGHT IS YOUR GIFT,
YOUR SPIRIT, YOUR SOUL.
IT GUIDES ALL YOUR
FOOTSTEPS
AND WILL
KEEP YOU
WHOLE.

I'll walk by
your side and
help you grow
strong,
while your light
gives you peace
when all else goes wrong.

DREAM BIG LITTLE ONE,
YOUR LIFE LIES AHEAD,
AS SLEEP BRINGS YOU COMFORT
FROM YOUR OWN TINY BED.

You'll wake in the morning, your light fixed and true and know that you're loved, whatever you do!